Gavin's Incredible World Of Beetles

By Crystal M. Gomez

Illustrated by Eloy Claudio

Crystal Gomez
El Cajon, CA
Printed in the United States of America

Illustrated by Eloy Claudio

ISBN-13: 978-0692969168
ISBN-10: 0692969160

Acknowledgements

A special thanks to teachers, Mr. Nelson, Mr. Avalos and Miss Simpson at Burbank Elementary in San Diego. Your fourth and fifth grade students are the best listeners!

First Edition: (November 2017)
10 9 8 7 6 5 4 3 2 1

Dedication

For every child who has ever been bullied.

G avin is being mean to beetles. He treats them like toys. Sometimes he's a downright bully. However, all bullies have a lesson to learn sooner or later.

"EWWW," Lindy squirmed, "Don't pull the wings!"
Gavin rolled his eyes. "It's just a beetle."
"You're hurting it," she said. "How would you like it to break your arms?"
"Don't be silly," he grinned. "Beetles can't hurt me."
Lindy ran from his room. "Mom…Gavin's being mean to bugs."
"They're beetles," Gavin shouted. "Not bugs."

"**D**on't worry," Gavin told his friends. "I won't break its wings. I'm going to make it fly like a kite." He wrapped string around the shiny green beetle's legs and let go. It buzzed toward the ceiling louder than his electric tooth brush. Benny and George watched with excitement.

"Can I hold it?" Benny asked.

Gavin held tight. "What will you give me?"

"I don't have anything," said Benny.

Gavin yanked the string. "Then you can't hold Greeny."

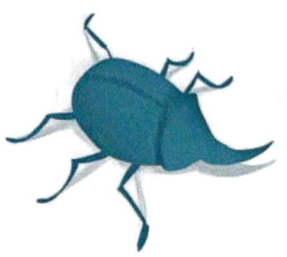

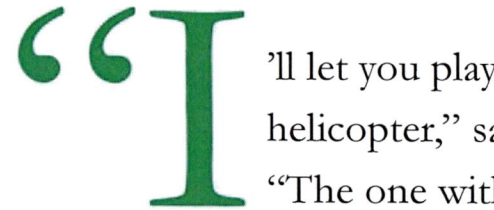

"**I**'ll let you play with my little brother's helicopter," said George.

"The one with the remote control?"

Gavin handed him the string. "Here, give it a try." The beetle zoomed high above their heads.

"Please give me a turn." Benny begged.

Gavin shook a jar of ladybugs. He laughed as their tiny bodies tossed against the glass.

"I'll let you hold my ugly, smelly stink beetle if you bring over your sister's hamster."

"**S**he won't let me take Whiskers out of the house," said Benny.

"No hamster, no beetle." Gavin insisted.

"Ok," Benny sighed. "I'll try."

Gavin grabbed the string from George. "Time's up. You know what to do if you want to play with my beetles."

Both boys left in a hurry.

Gavin ran through the room tugging the string as if he really was flying a kite. Up the beetle flew and down he pulled. Then, 'WHACK!' Gavin hit the wall and fell flat on his back.

"Ow." He rubbed his head. "Who turned out the lights?"

"Open your eyes," someone said.

"Who's there?" Gavin called.

"Open your eyes and find out."

Gavin opened his eyes and saw a
giant… green…

…beetle!

"Remember me?" it said. "I'm Greeny."

Gavin looked around. "Where am I?"

"You're in the World of Beetles. It's time to teach you a lesson."

"Oh no," Gavin trembled. "Please don't break my arms!"

"Don't be ridiculous,"
said a large ladybug.
"Who are you?" Gavin asked.
"I'm your teacher, Miss Lucy.
Welcome to your 'No Bullies' lesson."
"I'm not a bully," said Gavin.
The ladybug took notes. "We'll see about that."

R hino Rex sat him in front of a blackboard.

"Read the board please," Miss Lucy said.
Gavin read, "BULLIES…"

1) Are forceful and demanding
2) Make fun of others
3) Cause fear.

Miss Lucy asked, "Do you do any of these things?"
"Sometimes, I guess," Gavin mumbled. "That doesn't mean I'm a bully does it?"
"When we *act* like a bully, we *are* a bully. It's important to know how others feel when treated this way. Greeny, tell Gavin how you felt when he made you fly like a kite."

G

reeny said. "I felt frustrated and angry."

Gavin was surprised, "I thought you liked to fly."
"Not when I'm forced to. How would you like to be
pulled through the air at the end of a string?"
"Sounds fun to me," said Gavin.
"You're not afraid of getting hurt?"
"Hmm," Gavin paused. "On second thought…maybe
not."

A long legged beetle crawled forward.

"I'm Stuey Stink Beetle. I felt embarrassed when you called me ugly and smelly. Guys like me get teased a lot. We just need a chance to show you what we can do. Watch this."

Stuey did a headstand. Gavin stepped back.

"Relax," said Stuey. "I only spray my stinky-ness in emergencies."

"You sure have a strong head," Gavin said.

Stuey felt glad to get a compliment.

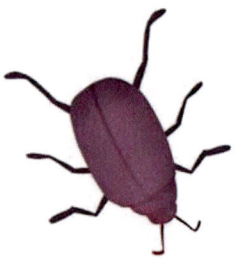

T wo small ladybugs stood together.

"We felt scared when you shook us in the jar."
A bright light shined and Gavin turned around.
"Speaking of jars, how would you liked to be locked in one all day?"
"What are you doing here?" Gavin said. "Fireflies aren't beetles."
"According to Google we are," said Fanny Firefly. "And I speak for beetles everywhere. None of us likes to be bullied."

G avin put his head down. "I didn't mean to hurt anyone. I was just having fun. Never thought I'd be a bully."

"Bullies aren't always someone else," said Miss Lucy. "Sometimes we need to look at ourselves."

"She's right," Greeny nodded. "And what does it mean when we act like a bully?"

"We are a bully." Gavin answered.

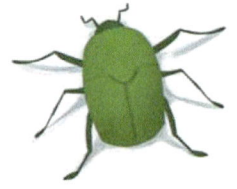

S tuey said, "Don't feel bad little guy. The good news is; you learned your lesson. That means you passed the class."

"Congratulations!" the group cheered.

Miss Lucy wrote one last word. "Say this three times with your eyes shut and you can go."

Gavin read, "Oz-Ka-Booey. What does that mean?"

"It means, **No Bullies**," said Greeny.

Gavin closed his eyes."Oz-Ka-Booey, Oz-Ka…"

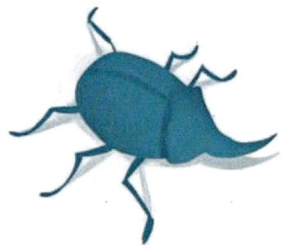

"**O**z-Ka Whooey?" someone said. Gavin opened his eyes. George stared down at him.

"Why are you on the floor? I brought my brother's helicopter."

"Take it back." Gavin said. He scooped up all his beetles and ran across the room.

"What are you doing?" George yelled.

Gavin opened the window and set the beetles free.

"Oz-Ka-Booey," he waved. "Oz-Ka-Booey."

BEETLE FUN FACTS

MISS LUCY: Lady Bug

These little cuties are a farmers best friend.
They eat harmful pests that destroy crops.
And they aren't colorful for nothing. Their red
spotted bodies warn predators to stay away!

FANNY: Firefly

Fireflies are unique. Their bodies produce
light that is the most efficient in the world.
They use their light to communicate with each
other.

GREENY: Fig Beetle

Fig Beetles are found in Southern California
and Mexico. Some say their metallic bodies
look like miniature aliens. Their sturdy wings
make a loud buzz. Watch out! They have poor
eyesight and often crash into humans.

STUEY: Stink Beetle

Another name for this beetle is Clown Bug. When threatened they really do stand on their heads and spray a smelly odor into the air.

RHINO REX: RHINOCEROS BEETLE

These are the strongest known animals on the planet. If they were human they could lift three Pro Wrestlers in the air…at the same time! They are also called Hercules Beetles. No Kidding.

BEETLES REALLY ARE INCREDIBLE…

STAY TUNED FOR GAVIN'S NEXT WORLD OF ADVENTURE…

Made in the USA
San Bernardino, CA
14 November 2017